The Kindness Response

The Kindness Response

Rabbi Lance J. Sussman Ph.D.

Published by Tablo

Table of Contents

"The highest form of wisdom is kindness." Brachot 17a

Dedicated to my family

and to all who have

taken care of me.

Preface

Several years ago, my mother sent me a box of papers from my childhood. I did not open the box until this summer and was surprised to see some poetry I had written as a little boy. In High School I joined the Poetry Club and during my college years studied poetry with the late Prof. Sanford (Sandy) Pinsker at Franklin & Marshall who helped sharpen my ability both to read and write poetry. I became an occasional poet, never fully concentrating on writing poems but also not totally abandoning poetry either.

On November 3, 2020, I had emergency heart surgery. As part of the healing process, I unwittingly intensified my writing poetry in gratitude to those who saved my life and supported me in the harrowing days which followed. In the hospital, I was deeply moved by the constant kindness of the healthcare professionals and my family members who helped me back to life. I saw in them a "kindness response" to life which I always knew existed but now appreciated as the core value of what it means to be a human being.

This slim book mostly includes poems written in the wake of my brush with death at the age of 66, events of the last two years and a few pieces reflecting on previous experiences. I hope it adequately expresses my gratitude to those who took care of me in my hour of need and helps others see the need for kindness in everything we do in the hospital, on the street, and at home.

Finally, I want to thank my daughter, Chana Sussman, for overseeing this project and Sarah Demers for the original artwork on the cover.

Rabbi Lance J. Sussman Ph.D.

January 17, 2021

The Kindness Response

May we be healed by those who attend to us.

May their experience, knowledge and kindness help restore our bodies and spirits.

May the genius of modern science work hand-in-hand with the ancient wisdom of the human heart.

May the doctors, nurses and attendants who treat us bring all their powers of person to our bed sides with focus and devotion.

May the love and concern of our families assure us that life has meaning and deep purpose.

May the messages of friends from near and far bring us solace and hope and remind us of the beauty of interdependence.

May our own fears dissolve in the sea of love which washes us with the balm of loving reassurance.

May the prayers of our hearts, our youth and age give us strength to carry on.

May the transcendent eternal love inherent in the universe lift our spirits and keep us strong in times of darkness.

May the stars, sun and rainbows drawn by the children in our lives help us to heal and strive to reach the tomorrows of health and happiness.

May we be healed and resolve to bring healing and comfort to others in the days ahead when we are well again.

May we know that the power of love is with us wherever we go and will always be the north star of our lives.

Grateful

At this precise moment

as our season of Thanksgiving begins

I am grateful for so many things and blessings

I am unsure I can list them all

but feel compelled to share as many of them as possible with you.

I am grateful for all those who have taken care of me

from the beginning of my life until now.

I am grateful for the doctors, nurses and hospital workers

who worked tirelessly to keep me alive

and return me to the fullness of life in recent days.

I am grateful for their knowledge, skill and experience

but most all, for their passion to heal the body

and for their compassion to mend the soul

and restore a semblance of peace to my mind.

I am grateful for the indefatigable stream of love

coursing through my family and into my being.

I am grateful for their guardianship through the long nights of uncertainty

and the evasive dawns waiting for renewed hope

that we endured together

recognizing full well that no amount of gratitude

will ever truly be sufficient or equal to their faithful devotion.

I am grateful for all my friends, near and far,

who made their presence felt in my hour of need.

I am grateful for every card, good wish, bouquet of flowers and donation.

I am grateful for their discretion and willingness to give me the time and space

I needed to heal and regain my strength.

I am grateful there is still abundant love for those still in their struggles

for life and deep in their own battles for continued existence.

I am grateful for the autumn colors which have repainted the canvass of the world

in the windows through which I now see the world.

I am grateful for the fallen leaves and their message of the endless cycle of life and renewal.

I am grateful for the waves, the sand and the sea and their promise of a better tomorrow

I eagerly wait to see again.

I am grateful for my country and its ever-renewing ability to return to
its founding aspirations

despite its many trials and tribulations.

I am grateful for my faith which is the candle of my soul

in good times and in bad

always lit and warm in my heart.

I am grateful to the Source of life and hope

the Keeper of eternal memories,

the Guarantor of all tomorrows

whose very presence proclaims that simply "to be" is good.

I am grateful for all these and more

and eager to offer my humble thanks

in this season of thanksgiving.

Please whisper with me a thank you

for all our blessings - personal, shared and eternal.

Prayer

Sometimes prayer is best read aloud

in fine verse

and well edited prose.

Sometimes prayer is best sung

with full voice

carrying the intention of the soul

from our inner selves

to the higher realms of existence

Sometimes prayer is best left in silence

where only the heart speaks

and listens to itself

where everything which needs to be said

and often cannot be said

is said silently

without uttering a single sound.

What's Next

What's next?

It's hard to know

when you can't see around the corner of time

or control your boat

in the rough seas of life

and can't see land or

beyond the next breaking wave

and your sails are down

and your motors are cut.

What's next?

It's hard to know

when you have lost a loved one

and have never really been alone before

without the usual sounds and smells

that makes their place in you life

complete.

What's next?

It's hard to know

when you are living in something called a pandemic

and watch too much news

and walk six feet away

from the nearest human being

who also doesn't know

what's next.

What's next?

I wish I knew more about tomorrow than today

to regain a sense of control

over the expanding unknown

which compromises our self contained

places of sanctuary

where we live and try to sleep

not knowing

what's next.

What's next

when hope is reduced

to an inner whisper

that fades

but doesn't quite disappear

clinging to the belief

that what is ok is possible

and we can arrive there

after what happens

next.

Family

They call us the nuclear family

but we are not protons, electrons or neutrons.

We are just people

living in relationship with one another

sometimes connected by DNA,

others linked by promises and vows

of different types

from marriage to adoption.

We are family.

and when just one of our electrons goes out of orbit

and our atom of family love is disrupted

and our wholeness as people is instantly broken by illness, disease or loss;

an instant and universal explosion of nuclear family energy is released,

as big as the big bang itself,

and waves of love, energy and light

go forth from our core

from our tiny nuclear family

and fill the whole universe with light and love

until the atom of our nuclear family is stable again

and retakes its quiet place,

among all the other billions of

nuclear families

and a universe of quiet love is restored

and we become one again

in a cosmos of perfect harmony.

Alone

My natural habitats are busy houses

filled with noisy children, chaos and pets

and offices bristling with work,

streams of new people and an abundance of problems

punctuating life on a constant basis.

Outside are the familiar cities which frame our existence

with their culture, economy and relentless noise

sidewalks defining life

with their cacophony in straight lines of finitude.

Perhaps for the ancient Greeks there was malevolence in chaos,

the swirl of people and events my soul needs.

Nor am I a modern Buddha who seeks the quiet of mindfulness

from a world which seems to overwhelm me

like a late night disco

with constant lightening strikes of life piercing laser beams.

The strange thing is that I need the noise

of daily life and want it to surround me.

I am home in the world of endless activity

and dread the quiet which smothers the sound of

life whirling all around me.

I am not built to be alone

to be left without companionship

to sit by a lake by myself

without human company

for endless hours

or be at home without the tumult of family life.

Silent walls are my enemy

they are my soul's prison

and I fear the unknown term they impose.

on my life when I am simply by myself.

I need the noise of life

even when I cannot hear it

and surrounds me

offering protection from the aloneness

which attacks my soul and peace of being

I can only find when I am not alone.

Sleep

I don't understand sleep

or where we go when our world disappears.

I dread the long hours of darkness

alone and unsure of how to spend my time

in the solitude of the night.

I am surprised by awakening

not knowing I had slept

and remain engaged in my dreams

not knowing where they came from

or why people I know

but who don't know each other

spoke to one another.

I wait for the dawn and the new day

and the safety of consciousness

when sleep is a thing of the past

that didn't really happen

and wonder about the next day

when the challenge of sleep again waits for me

in the dark with the uncompromising reality of night

and its shadows of uncertainty.

My Mommy is Here

Many days, at the end of day

I stand by the preschool fence where the 2 and 3-year old's play.

They are busy with sand and trucks and one another.

and then one says, "My mommy is here"

and they stop playing and their arms go up

and they jump into mommy's loving arms

and she kisses her children

and the world is one.

Forget the toys and the kick balls

and the fun and the buzz of the playground,

Mommy is here and I am going home.

and for that moment

that's all there is in heaven and on earth.

When I go home, I watch the news on the TV

I hear what I cannot accept.

I see what I cannot believe.

My country is taking children out of the hands of their moms and dads removing nursing infants from their mother's soft embrace

and putting them in cages

but they say resorts

of course, it doesn't matter

none of those kids can say "my mommy is here"

only strangers and procedures and

government issued cots

for kids on ICE near our border.

Don't we remember the auctions where slaves once were sold,

where families were ripped apart?

Don't we remember the transports which separated

Jewish kids from their moms and dads

along the tracks across Europe from Amsterdam to Zagreb?

How simple, how natural the words children say

when their mommy is here.

Is it possible my country cannot hear them?

Is it possible for me to sleep when I hear them

and then close my eye to reality?

At The Border

At the border of our country

we have arrived at the line between right and wrong

as a nation and as a people.

On the other side, are people yearning to be free

who are labeled as animals and criminals

as they flee from violence in their homelands

and abandon their homes, their extended families, friends and way of life.

At the border of our country

are rivers of discontent, confusion, anger and worry.

Invisible walls of hatred block the way to the USA

and deserts of danger make long passages treacherous.

At the border of our country

families are trapped between savage coyotes and misled ICE men

who make the journey to freedom

perilous and insecure.

At the border of our country

there is no turning back to poverty

and the nightmares of brutal violence, rape, torture and death.

At the border of our country

is the last faint hope for relief

against all the odds.

At our border, our leaders no longer

can hear the revolutionary cry of

"Give me Liberty or give me death"

and then plan a fate worse from death

by ripping children from their mothers' arms

and detaining them alone

at a tender age

in American concentration camps.

At the border of my country

the light of human decency is flickering,

caught between our ideals and our worst impulses as a nation.

At the border of my country

there is a line in the sand.

On one side is the light of tomorrow

on the other, is the darkness of oppression and private anguish.

At the border of our nation,

we wait with anxiety

and want to know which side of the line of humanity

our country will make its final stand.

God Bless America: A Protest

God bless America

ideals that I love

through the gas and the glass

in the night of our broken laws

from our cities to the White House

to the police stations

burned and charred,

God bless America

land filled with scars

God bless America

its streets filled with youth

crying for justice to its leaders

who decided long ago to be deaf.

God bless America

whose promise is sublime

while its people resist sinking

into the depths of hypocrisy

and crime.

God bless America

land I revere

with its ownerless Bibles

and its prayer-less moments

filled with contempt for humanity.

God bless America

land that I love

still praying for justice and for hope

and the promise of its original dreams.

We Shall Prevail

We are living in a strange moment,

nothing we have ever experienced before.

Some of us have seen war

and pressed hard on the muddy floors of foxholes.

Some of us have faced illness

and watched the drip of IV's restore life in our veins.

Some of us have lost our life savings

and wonder if just enough will still be enough

to live our lives.

All of us have lost loved loves

and felt the finality of death sting our souls.

But now we are at an unprecedented moment,

Not some of us, but all of us.

Not a recitation of Passover plagues

or a lesson about a 14th century catastrophe

with the Angel of Death leading children and rats

through the streets of dying medieval cities.

We are not in the Philadelphia of the Yellow Fever

or the pandemic of 1918 during the First World War

which viciously cut down young lives like silent machine guns

with bullets forged from bacteria and medical ignorance.

We are living in a strange, unprecedented moment

unfortified by the Olympian fortresses of modern science

which has yet to create a synthetic shield to a microscopic virus

that penetrates all human armor.

We are living a moment of growing, personal isolation

increasingly instructed to self-isolate,

to withdraw from society and sports and entertainment

and even simple, familiar acts of faith.

No one is saying it out loud but the message is clear:

"You must be strong alone,

you need to be disciplined and smart,

and cautious and vigilant."

Tradition teaches to live with a pure heart,

science says to live with clean hands.

Now is the time to collect our inner selves

and to be strong alone

until the time comes again

when we can be strong together.

Until then

until that day

let us resolve that we shall prevail.

A New Birth of Freedom

They came by the thousands

in a hundred cities and more

with their cellphones

and skateboards,

wearing their armor

of T-shirts and political slogans.

They marched

they knelt

they laid down in the streets.

they held up their cardboard signs

and spray painted patriotism

for the press and police to see

and would not go home

unafraid of being handcuffed

until all were free.

We thought they were hypnotized

by their video games and apps

and didn't care about anything

but parties and unearned vacations

and strange expensive drinks with clever names

while we, an older generation,

who believed that demonstrations

were a thing of the past,

watched on our cable televisions

wearing our COVID 19 masks,

a new birth of freedom and hope

in the land of brave.

Thank you to a million leaderless kids

for saving our country's soul

for relighting the torch of liberty

for future generations

who will remember these blue jean warriors on bicycles and skates

who kept the promise of America alive until dawn's early light.

Buchenwald

Our purpose was to make a statement

about German and Jewish kids

standing together in the middle of a concentration camp.

The hospital used for medical experimentation stood to our left

and execution stalls stood to our right.

A sea of putrid barracks

had been flattened into a sea of gravel

where silence had replaced stench and fear.

They stood there in a circle

and held hands.

All the words and poems and songs they prepared

were ready in their heads and hearts

to be shared and conjoined.

But then there was silence.

they just stood there

in the middle of Buchenwald

and said nothing

about everything

called life.

Stratford-upon-Avon

I didn't know that Shakespeare's grave

was in a church

in a modest frame

off center and unimposing.

In my imagination

the master of the stage

should have had a monumental marker

equal to his body of work

reflecting the whole of human existence.

Sanctuaries I suppose

can be of any size

or state of grandeur,

their holiness not defined by an imposing monument

but by the essence

of their words and deeds.

Kaddish (Remember)

We all have universes of memory and pain

that exist without competition among mourners

without claims of personal exceptionalism.

Death alone levels the playing field of life.

We are all the same

in our brokenness and in our anger.

We are equal in our aching,

in our incompleteness

in our desire to hear, to see

to touch just one more time,

Like a great weather system

death slowly but completely engulfs the environment around us,

an afternoon thunder storm,

which roars through our lives

and leaves debris and brokenness all around.

Like a shadow cast on a quiet, sunny afternoon

by just one dark cloud

death comes into our lives

and redefines who we are and what we will become.

As sure as night follows day

as sure as tomorrow itself

death comes into our lives.

Death is a regular visitor

but an unwelcome guest in our lives.

Inevitable, uncontrollable,

death is always disarming

always complete

always more powerful than we are

until we can regain control

over some portion of who we were.

In time, the dead come back to us

in dreams

in artifacts they left behind

in pictures

in memories

in the smell of soup and holiday meals.

in the new good times when they should have been at the table

but aren't

yet still are there

still with us

in every breath, in every step, in every thought.

In truth the dead never leave us.

They are in the wind

in the first kiss on a new baby's cheek

in our words

and in the silence between our words

where they live forever.

Until Then

Until then

until the day when we really have to say

goodbye forever,

until then

let us live tomorrow as the promise

of what we still hope to achieve today.

Until then

fill us with the love we need like oxygen

to breathe life fully.

Until then

open our eyes

so that we may see clearly the beauty

and the love that has surrounded us

from our very beginnings as people

to our present struggles

and will always live within us.

Until then

may we live in the eternity

of the blessings we enjoy at this moment

in peace and in love.

About the Author

Lance J. Sussman, Ph.D., is an historian of American Jewish History, college professor, Chair of the Board of Governors of Gratz College, Melrose Park, PA and the senior rabbi at Reform Congregation Keneseth Israel (KI) located in Elkins Park, PA. A trained historian of the American Jewish experience that he has taught at Princeton University, Binghamton University (SUNY) and Hunter College, NY.

Lance J. Sussman is the author of numerous books and articles including: *Isaac Leeser and the Making of American Judaism* (1995) and *Sharing Sacred Moments* (1999), and a co-editor of *Reform Judaism in America: A Biographical Dictionary and Sourcebook* (1993) and *New Essays in American Jewish History* (2009). Since 2010 he has also published articles on Judaism and art. This is his first published book of poetry.